Catholic to the Core
Spiritual Fitness To Transform Your Life

Bruce Baumann

Tom,

God Bless + always stay
Catholic to the Core!

— Bruce B.

ISBN-13: 978-1721187379

CONTENTS

DEDICATIONS

To my beautiful wife Wendy. Twenty-five years of marital bliss and counting. I could not thank you enough for your unwavering love and support in everything I do.

To our son Bryce. What a fine, young man you have become. I pray that God will continue to bless and mold you in your seminary formation.

To our daughter Blair. You will always be my little hunny-bunny. I enjoy our deep conversations and am so grateful to have a daughter like you.

To my mom and dad, Carol and Dick and my sister Kim. I am eternally thankful for everything you have done for me throughout my life.

To all of our extended family members, friends and colleagues in ministry. Thank you for your prayers and encouragement in my faith journey.

Most of all to our Lord. May this book reflect your beauty, truth and love!

1 WAKE-UP CALL

Tom sank into his chair with a heaviness that was palpable. His long term girlfriend had abruptly severed their relationship. This is someone who had become his everything. His adoration of her was unmatched by anything else in his life – past or present. This cold shower moment had shaken him to his core. The foundation of Jennifer in his life was not only crumbling, but disintegrating with each passing moment.

This was not an impulsive or temporary bump in the road. No, this was a permanent goodbye. It had been coming on for a while and culminated in the discovery of her interest in another guy. This was no passing fad with a chance of an eventual reunion. The love of his life was gone...for good. That gut wrenching reality had taken hold of him allowing no opportunity for escape. No relief in sight. No glimmer of hope. No reason to get up in the morning. Just profound and utter despair.

When someone occupies that space, tired clichés and well-intentioned moral encouragement ring hollow and do not stand much chance of reaching their intended target. Sometimes the only loving thing to do is to offer your unconditional presence. That is what I attempted during that initial stage. I remained in his presence as his friend and journeyed with him in this place that contained so little light.

Tom and I eventually moved on from this chapter to a more neutral state of being. As guys sometimes best cope, we turned to physical activity – in our case, a rousing game of tennis. This was always one of our favorite past times. It got the blood flowing and in the friendly competitive spirit in which we played, it provided a brief respite from the pain that had shadowed him since the breakup.

After completing our day with a trip to the local pizza buffet, his mind was already starting to shift gears. While still feeling the sting, he became quite introspective. This is where I sensed the opening and produced perhaps an even bigger shock in his life. "How is your walk with the Lord?" I casually asked while we drank our soda. Tom looked at me as if I had suddenly grown two heads. "What?"he said incredulously. I repeated calmly "How is your walk with the Lord?" Sensing he was not grasping my intention, I rephrased "You know, how is your faith life going?" That seemed to strike more of a chord and he began to open up.

For the next two hours, time stood still. We were oblivious to everything around us. There could have been a tornado bearing down on us and I am not sure we would have deviated from our conversation. The Holy Spirit was stirring within both of us in this evangelical exchange.

Tom was like many of us (me included) in that he grew up Catholic, called himself Catholic, identified as Catholic, but never really got it. I am reminded of the blockbuster movie Titanic. I was a parish youth minister in suburban Minneapolis when this movie came out. As was the case all over the country, teenagers were going crazy over this film. Seeing it once or twice was not enough – they were circling back to the theatre ten or twelve times. This did not make sense to me. We all knew the ending – the ship sinks. Where was the drama? The suspense? The intrigue? What was it about this movie that was fascinating so many people – especially teenagers? After four months of speculation, my wife and I had a friend watch our newborn baby boy while we trekked off to the local theatre to find out what the fuss was all about.

After three hours of riveting suspense, I got it. It was the story. We all knew the facts, but we never really humanized it – never personalized it - never connected with it ourselves until that moment. Even the movie itself alluded to this when the captain of the expedition admitted that he had ate and drank nothing but Titanic for the years leading up to the exploration and yet, he had never let it in. The story, the emotions, the people, the events. Once he did, his perspective did a 180.

It is similar to our spiritual journey. Many of us know about Catholicism and we know about God, but do we really <u>know</u> Him? Do we let Him in? The majority of Catholics keep God at arm's length. This is where Tom was at this moment, but the rays of conviction and hope were starting to penetrate his heart.

I shared my own faith journey with him – all of its joys, doubts and struggles. My faith was far from perfect, but it had entered a much different realm from where I was before and from where Tom had been up until that point.

After this amazing exchange had taken place, I concluded by challenging him to commit his life to Jesus, go to Reconciliation and to begin anew. He did not do so at that moment and that was OK. In order for this to be authentic, he had to take this step on his own. You could see grace flooding his soul as his countenance was evolving before my eyes. The despair that hung so heavy on him before was evaporating like the early morning fog when the sun starts rising. In this case, the Son was hard at work within his soul. Tom was not only smiling and really looking forward to the future, but he was already recognizing that this is what he needed all along and Jennifer cutting him off was probably the biggest blessing to have happened to him.

Tom's journey is not all that different from many of ours. I think most of us have tried to live our lives outside of God's influence. If questioned on a census or school survey, we probably would have checked the Catholic box, but what does that really mean?

My last name is Baumann which is German in origin. I have never actually been to Germany. I do not speak German. I do not eat German food. I do not even drink beer – the Oktoberfest people would be disappointed in me ☺. Clearly, I am German in name only. That is exactly how we can be with our Catholicism. In varying degrees, we are Catholic in name only. It might be something we wear as a badge of honor, but carries no real significance in our life.

This is where we need to recognize one very important truth. God wants all of us. Not just lip service or a name or a random thought or the occasional cameo appearance at Mass.

I wrestled a long time with the idea of writing a book like this. There are lots of great Catholic books and resources out there, many of which I have been edified by myself. However, I still felt compelled to produce this one in the way in which it is presented. The title says it all. I want to cut to the core – get to the essence of Catholicism. My goal is to provide a blueprint for true spiritual transformation.

If you are really on fire for your faith or you have drifted far away or you find yourself somewhere in between, this book, this process could be life changing for you. The key to this transformation does not lie in reading the words or understanding the concepts. No, like anything else you have to act upon this new found knowledge. Therefore, as much as possible, I have included concrete and specific action steps. Depending on where you are in the journey or your own life circumstance, you will have to prayerfully discern when and how you implement these ideas.

The bottom line is that we need to move – period. Remaining stagnant is not an option. We are called to continually learn and grow no matter how young or old. That is the beauty of our faith – it is infinite and eternal. Are you ready to embrace the challenge? To go deeper than ever before? To experience the transformative power of God? If so, let's get to it!

2 SOUL ASSESSSMENT

When you first sign up at the gym, they will usually offer to do an initial assessment of where you are at in your fitness level. This could include weighing you, doing a body fat analysis, having you take endurance tests, etc. Doing so not only provides a baseline to measure your future progress, but also helps to forge a realistic game plan moving forward. Perhaps the biggest benefit is that it can serve as wake-up call to the true state of health we may find ourselves in. There are very few individuals that actually enjoy this process. How many times do people put off scheduling their annual physical? Not many of us like to face the facts and yet, that is the first step towards health.

Our souls are no different. They can be every bit as complex and varied as our physical health. We need to dive beneath the surface and see what is going on within our hearts and mind. Are you ready to take the plunge?

Rate yourself on a scale of 1 to 10 with 1 being almost nonexistent and 10 being super strong.

My relationship with God _____

Time spent in prayer _____

Attendance and participation in Sunday Mass _____

Reception of the Sacrament of Reconciliation _____

Reading the Bible _____

Actively serving others _____

Seeking God's will in my life _____

Attending Bible studies or formation groups at my parish _____

Going on spiritual retreats _____

Sharing my faith with others _____

Now add up your scores. Are you in the A range (90 and above?). How about a B (80-89)? Perhaps you scored a respectable C (70-79). Or maybe you find yourself far below that.

Obviously, this is a very simplistic assessment. It is not scientific or all inclusive. One's spiritual state cannot easily be quantified. Perhaps you really are a solid B, but because of your humbleness, you ranked yourself lower thus generating a worse grade. In this case, you should get extra credit for your humility bumping you up to the next level.

There are many variables to consider here and most everything is relative. If you ranked yourself in comparison to Adolph Hitler, you probably came out pretty well. If Mother Teresa was the standard to which you had in mind, you might have ranked yourself much lower. Here is the bottom line. We are all in need of improvement. Every one of us falls short of the glory of God which is why we need Jesus as our savior. If we think we can be good and holy on our own, we are doomed to failure. What we need and what this is intended to do is to take a good, hard and honest look at ourselves so we can make the necessary lifestyle choices to allow God's grace to transform our minds and renew our hearts.

What I am doing here is holding up a mirror for you to gaze into. This is designed to help you reflect, dig deep and discover the true state of your soul. If you died today, would you feel comfortable with what you are presenting to the Lord? Are you really living each day the best you possibly can? Are you fulfilling God's destiny for your life? If the answer is no to any of these questions, then I strongly suggest you forge ahead. This could be the very thing to get you on track.

Many years ago, I remember getting a call from a very good friend of mine. We were living in separate states at the time and just catching up. Matt was lamenting that his faith life was not going so well. He was in college and struggling with time management. Matt valued his faith a great deal and was the first to tell you that Jesus was number one in his life. I inquired further about his dilemma. He explained that with work and school, his quiet time with God was almost nonexistent. It was Sunday evening when he called and he was going to be doing homework most of the night and by the time he was done, he would be too tired to read his Bible or pray.

I asked Matt if he could tell me what he had done that day. He said that after sleeping in, he watched the Minnesota Vikings game. This was his favorite team. Since he was in fantasy football, he then would flip channels back and forth between two other NFL games to see how his players were doing. He ate dinner and now he was talking to me. It became very clear to me as I challenged him, "Matt, you say that God is number one in your life, but he certainly wasn't today. Football was your god today." This jarred him as he asked "What do you mean?" I explained that instead of watching six hours of football, he could have been doing his homework which would have freed up plenty of time in the evening for prayer and Bible study. Of course, an even better plan would have been to reverse it by setting aside the quiet time early in the day. Either way, it would have made a real difference in how his day went.

If we are honest, we do this a lot. If we were to analyze what we spend our time, energy and money on, we will find that God is oftentimes way down on the totem pole. We reap what we sow. It is no wonder many of us are floundering in life. Jesus said to build our lives on Him – the rocky foundation. Instead, we are trying to do so on quicksand.

Going to Mass on Sunday is great and absolutely vital in our walk with Him, but it is only the beginning. The word Mass stems from the Latin word missa which loosely means sent. In other words, we go to Mass to be filled with Christ to then be sent out in the world (mission). Isn't that interesting? Most of us do not view Mass that way. Usually, we see it as something we go to as a destination – a final destination.

We need to examine our intentions as it relates to our life at church. I will hear people say (and I have said or thought myself before), "I like to go to the Saturday evening Mass to get it out of the way". Or people will share that they enjoy the early morning Mass so they have the rest of the day to themselves. We have heard that so much it doesn't even raise a red flag anymore.

The practical side of me says that makes good sense. After all, they are making Mass a priority by getting it in (which is good), but the thinking that surrounds it is troubling. God – Mass – our faith become a checklist – an obligation that can be marked off so we can move on to the "good stuff."

Do you sense God stirring in your soul? Is your conscience feeling some conviction by the Holy Spirit? Does life seem out of whack? Are you sick and tired of feeling sick and tired? Do you yearn for purpose, meaning and fulfillment? Do you want your faith to be more than a checklist item? Perhaps your faith is in a good spot, but you crave more depth and you want to proceed to the next level. Wherever you are, it is time for the next step – commitment.

3 MAKING A COMMITMENT

This is one of the shortest chapters in the book, but it may be the most important. You and I have both witnessed human nature first hand time and time again. This amazing ability to procrastinate. To say or believe one thing and to do something else. Someday, I will get in shape. Someday, I will be more spiritual. Someday, I will reconcile with my family members. God has a revelation for you. That someday is today.

Reading a spiritual book like this is nice, but if nothing changes because of it, it remains just that – nice. Nice does not change anyone. It does not involve conversion or transformation. It simply is. That is why when people characterize Jesus as a nice guy, I want to scream. Was he kind, compassionate and loving? Of course, but he was far more than nice. Jesus was transformative in every sense of the word.

God wants to transform us as well. If the Holy Spirit is inspiring you in any way as you read this book, then you <u>must</u> act. Anything less is what the Church calls a sin of omission. That is when there is something that you should be doing (e.g. praying, serving, etc.) and you choose not to do it. This can be just as grievous as sins of commission - doing things that we should not be doing (e.g. lying, stealing, etc.).

Now, what that action is depends on each individual. We are all on a different part of the journey. Not all of us are called to be or act like Mother Teresa. Only Mother Teresa could fulfill the call that God put on her life. We are all in different stages and circumstances. In the scriptural Body of Christ analogy, we are all different parts that play varying roles in building up the Kingdom of God.

One thing we do have in common is the universal call to holiness. All of us have this by virtue of our baptismal anointing.

Reading this book cannot merely be an intellectual pursuit. No, it must be an encounter with the living Lord. God wants to do great things in your life. He does not want your soul to be out of shape or spiritually flabby. He does not want you to go through the motions anymore. This is your opportunity to change course, to do a 180, to go deep – far deeper than you have ever gone before.

In order for this to happen, I need you to take two actions steps right now. Do not read one more page until this happens. If it takes you five minutes to do these steps – fantastic. If it takes you five days or five weeks, that is OK too. This needs to be your own authentic journey. No one is there to watch you. This is between you and God. Here goes...

Step 1 – Pray.

Simply ask the Holy Spirit to open up your mind, heart and soul like never before. Pray that Christ will touch and transform you at a level you have not experienced before. Ask for the intercession of all the saints and angels (especially our Blessed Mother Mary) that God will reveal His plan for your life in very real and tangible ways.

Step 2 – Commit

Whatever conviction or insight that you receive from the Lord, I want you to commit to God that you will indeed take action. You won't put it off. You won't say "someday." Don't get me wrong. We all know that meaningful change takes time. These things do not happen overnight, but the key is to begin and to stick with it.

I am a big resolution guy. I love making them and at least trying to keep them. This is particularly true at two junctures in the calendar year - New Year's Day and Ash Wednesday. Many people love to make New Year's or Lenten Resolutions. If nothing else, it gives us the illusion that we will somehow be different.

The most popular New Year's Resolution by far (at least in the developed countries) revolves around physical fitness and health. This takes the form of losing weight, getting in shape, eating better, etc. Fitness memberships peak at the beginning of January. Most everyone usually does quite well out of the gate. However, after a couple of weeks, attrition is already setting in. By the end of January, people are starting to give up and give in. Events and holidays like the Super Bowl and Valentine's Day start to punch holes in the dike. After a while, water continues to pour through and by spring the dam has completely burst for most. They attempt to try again the following year, but it usually ends the same way.

Why is this? Why can't we stay the course? Well, there are a variety of reasons, but one of the main ones is our overall resolve. We have to make a commitment and stick to it no matter what. It does not mean that we are perfect. We will stumble and even fall. That is OK. The key is to get back up and to recommit. Therein lies the difference between those who talk the talk and those who walk the walk. No matter what the circumstances, you will commit to stick with the program – to stay the course. As the

Lord leads, you will follow. Not easy, but very simple.

If you have not done these two steps – then stop and put the book down. If you have indeed prayed and made your commitment to do whatever the Lord tells you, then it is time to journey forward. Let the adventure begin!

4 SPIRITUAL CLEANSING

With the persistent heat and sun that we receive in
Texas, my yard and flower beds can look pretty ugly
at times. Weeds and bushes grow wildly out of
control crowding out the grass and plants that I want
to bloom and flourish. Every now and then, these
areas need a good, strong purge. Lots of pruning,
pulling and digging – going deep to get at the very
roots so as to eliminate and eradicate. Once this
laborious and sometimes painful process is done, I am
then free to re-create my yard.

It is the same with God. His divine and majestic
energy makes us new. In order to let God's grace
create that masterpiece in our lives, we need to do
some purging. We have accumulated lots of junk and
allowed the weeds (sins) to grow and expand. We are
in need of a spiritual cleansing.

This is where that most wonderful sacrament that we call Reconciliation comes in (or oftentimes referred to as Confession or even Penance). One time, I was at a Protestant youth ministers' conference. My colleagues and I had gone to this event as undercover Catholics. Unless asked specifically what church we were associated with, our aim was to fly under the radar and to blend into the Protestant crowd. Some of our parents would lament that their kids wanted to go to XYZ church and wondered why they did not want to come to our Catholic youth programs. The answer to that lies in a conversation for another day. Suffice it to say that we were on a mission to discover the holy grail of youth ministry – to discover their secret formulas so that we too could have similar success with our youth programs.

What we found was that there was no magic bullet (of course) and that while Protestant youth ministry used to be way ahead of Catholic youth ministry, our Church had indeed caught up in this regard. The other churches struggled in the same areas we did and were essentially asking themselves very similar questions.

In fact, as we walked around and experienced the three day conference, a bizarre revelation was becoming apparent. Many of the Protestant churches were trying to reclaim vestiges of Catholic spirituality and practice. One glaring example of this was found off to the side in the "Healing Room." This was an optional activity whereby participants would enter and receive some kind of spiritual restoration. As one glanced into this space, you saw various healing stations where there would be two chairs facing one another with a candle and Bible nearby on a stand. There were pastors sitting in the one chair waiting for people to take turns sitting in the other chair opposite them. Once they sat down, the person would share their struggles and weaknesses. The pastor would provide some spiritual counseling/advice, pray over them and then send them on their way.

It was as obvious as anything we had seen there – they were trying to emulate the Sacrament of Reconciliation. It had the trappings of the Sacrament and I am sure some very good things came out of it, but it was still just a shell of what the ultimate healing really is. Like many other things, we are so incredibly blessed to have this sacrament available to us. There is really nothing quite like it. To know that we can confess our sins and that our sins are actually forgiven is an awesome realization. The priest acts in the person of Christ and God's love and forgiveness coming pour forth in our lives. Our souls are scrubbed clean. We are pure and undefiled. A new beginning. That fresh start we so desperately longed for has arrived. Complete freedom from the bondages of our sin. Now *that* makes for a very good day.

Prior to this new found freedom, there is a critical step that we must embark on first. It is called the examination of conscience. This is like our Soul Assessment except much more specific. We need to take a good, hard look in the mirror – up close and with all the lights on. This is where it can be humbling. We may not like what we see. Why in the world would we want others to see? Not only do we invite someone else in the room, but we go to great lengths to point out the very flaws we try so hard to cover up. Being completely honest is crucial to a thorough examination of our sins. Our goal is to eradicate all of the weeds that have taken root in our soul.

There are lots of great examination of conscience lists out there. I would suggest you find one that works well for you. By this, I mean where the questions are ones that you can relate to and the subsequent probing that results is challenging. Think of the examination as representing a really good set of garden tools. Questions, reflections and prayers that are pointed and insightful will prepare you for a greater awareness and openness to God's grace to work in and through you. The examination's power is felt not only in the reception of the Sacrament, but also as you move forward in the spiritual life. It provides a blueprint to help you steer away from those areas that lure you away from God. It helps you to avoid "the near occasion of sin."

Perhaps you have received the Sacrament of Reconciliation recently so you are ready to move on. If it has been a while (no matter how good you have been), it never hurts to have another cleansing. Make sure you partake in this wonderful instrument of God's grace.

If it has been a really long time since you have been to Reconciliation, you may have some (or a lot of) trepidation. What if the priest yells at me? What if I cannot remember everything? It can be so embarrassing or humiliating. Can't I just skip this part? Absolutely not. This is essential. The beautiful garden that God has planned for you will never happen until you allow Him to clean up your yard. Reconciliation restores our relationship with the Lord and frees up His grace to begin flowing freely within us once again.

Having worked for the Church for so long, I have heard many adults express these concerns about confessing to the priest. In reality, most priests will say that people's sins do not shock them like you think they would. Sadly, they hear many of the same things (usually worse) time and time again. It does not faze them. They are just glad you are there. Do not delay any longer. You will feel so much better.

5 WARMING UP

Congratulations! Your spiritual cleansing may have been one of the hardest steps. Now the fun begins – getting spiritually fit.

When I turned forty, I decided to pursue one of my bucket list items and that was to run a marathon. I have always been physically active and have enjoyed working out. As a kid, I spent most of my waking hours outdoors doing something physical. From street hockey and sledding in the winter to baseball and football in the summer, the neighborhood kids and I were continually engaged in some form of competitive sports. This continued into college where my roommate was into weightlifting/bodybuilding and I soon joined him on his daily treks to the local gym. I did gain the "freshmen fifteen," but it came in the form of increased muscle mass.

My passion for working out kept going once I got into my career although the motivation had shifted. I no longer was trying to impress the girls with my physique (which never worked anyway ☺). No, I liked the energy that working out gave me. As time wore on, this evolved into a more holistic motivation of overall health. My lifelong goal was (and still is) to be as strong and healthy as I can be so I can serve my family and those around me to the highest degree.

My fitness level at age forty was pretty good. There were two things that I could not do as well anymore. I could not run as fast and could not jump as high. Besides those two facets, I honestly felt just as good as when I was twenty (still do actually). However, even though I worked out regularly, I was not accustomed to long distance running. The most I would ever normally run is about three miles in the morning and this was only done maybe twice a week. I always tried to do a variety of exercises that included weight training and cardio.

Because of this, I was ill-prepared to run a marathon. First, running did not come naturally to me. I could do it, but it was more labor some for me than it was for others. I had friends who I jogged with and they bounded along effortlessly (or so it seemed) while I was struggling. As I already mentioned, I also was not conditioned to run long distances as I had not been doing so.

Even with these hurdles, I was intrigued with the idea of this new challenge. I knew that I could not just sign up for a marathon without proper training and that the process would have to be methodical. After surfing the internet to hear from the experts, I came up with a plan that would work for me and my schedule. I was not aiming for a certain time. I simply wanted to finish.

My plan was to start training six months before the event. I would continue my routine of running three to four miles a day a couple of times a week. Then on Saturday morning (early, when it was cool out), I would do my long run. My first week started with five miles. After a couple of weeks of doing that, I increased it to six. A couple more weeks would pass, I ran for seven. I remember that during this particular run, I was dying. It was one of those days where you feel like you do not have much energy. This was one of those fork in the road moments. The enormity of running a full marathon weighed on me. I thought if I am struggling with just seven miles, how could I possibly do almost four times that amount? The thought of that was overwhelming. I limped back home and did some soul searching. Did I want to continue with this crazy idea? No one would really care if I gave up now. It sure would save me from having to spend my Saturday mornings like this.

This is where the Holy Spirit intervened. I felt this conviction (still, small voice) that I should forge ahead. That somehow I needed this. It was time for me to break out of my comfort zone and to test my limits -to go beyond. So, I did.

An amazing thing happened. Seven miles turned into eight and eight turned into nine and ten was not too far behind. The first time I completed ten miles, I got home and marveled at what I had accomplished. TEN MILES. That was over twice the distance I had ever run before my marathon training. The surprising part is that it was not that difficult. Running ten miles this time was easier than running seven that other time. I had found my rhythm. My form was consistent and my breathing was more relaxed. More importantly, my mind was right.

They say that running long distances is more of a mental challenge than a physical one. I agree. Instead of thinking how hard it was, I would get lost in my thoughts. I spent a lot of time reflecting and praying for various people. Some days, I would end up praying three or four rosaries. For vast stretches, it was actually peaceful and life-giving.

In my newfound zealousness, I started increasing my lengths by two miles. This is where my knee started acting up. The only way to heal it was to rest. I ended up taking about six weeks off and then I was back to square one again. I honestly did not know if I was going to be able to do this or not. Will my endurance be enough? Will my knee become too injured to allow me to complete the race? Doubts and anxieties started creeping in again. I was also running out of training time.

Though a major setback, I knew I still had enough days to give it one more shot. This time, I was more prudent in my preparation and was careful not to push too hard or go too fast. Slow and steady wins the race or, at least in my case, it allowed me to enter the race.

My big day had finally arrived as I found myself alongside twenty thousand other hopeful and anxious participants. I did make one error in strategy that ended up affecting my performance. In my rush of excitement and adrenalin, I started off way too fast. I was feeling so good and energized that I ended up going at too strong of a pace out of the gate. I was passing everyone which only boosted my confidence. For the first eight or nine miles, I was on top of the world – cruising effortlessly through the course. This was going to be far easier than I ever thought.

That is when the dreaded "wall" reared its ugly head. I had heard about the phenomenon of hitting the wall, but people would mention this when talking about mile twenty or twenty-two or even twenty–

four. It was not supposed to happen at mile nine! I still had seventeen long miles to go. However, there it was in all its agonizing pain. When that last bit of adrenaline had worn off, the stark reality of my situation set in. Being this was my first marathon experience; I was hoping this was just a temporary set-back. I just needed to slow down. Unfortunately, that made things only worse. I found myself in a very tough spot. The more I slowed down, the harder it became to regain my form and yet I lacked the energy to do anything else. I had lost my momentum. Now it was just a matter of survival.

Spectators were very supportive. They were cheering me by name (which was on the front of our bibs) and saying things like "You are doing great" or "Keep going, you are almost halfway there." Even though they meant well and I appreciated them trying to help me, I was not in a good place to receive their support. I knew I was not doing well and the thought that I was only halfway through was like a kick in the gut. How would I ever make it to the end?

The next three hours may have been the longest of my life. Through sheer will and determination (and it took a lot of both), I did make it to the finish line. I vowed never to do another marathon ever again. I was a one and done kind of guy. Of course, I had to eat those words as well. Five years later, I ran another marathon with the goal of enjoying it more (which I did). After this last marathon, someone on the internet mentioned that running a marathon was equivalent to running the length of a football field – four hundred and sixty-six times. Yikes! Talk about daunting.

One of the lessons I learned in my marathoning experience was the importance of warming up. This is true anytime one works out. You do not begin by lifting the heaviest weight possible. That is a recipe for a major injury and setback. Your muscles need to warm up and be more limber. This is accomplished by several sets and reps with lighter weights. Once the blood starts flowing, your body is now ready for something more challenging.

It is similar with running a marathon. In terms of training, you must start slowly. You do not zoom from zero to twenty-six miles overnight. You need to build up endurance and strength.

The same can be said for the spiritual life. Many people who have drifted or never really been into their faith look at very active Catholics or Protestant Christians and think, "That could never be me." "I am not spiritual like them." For them, it is like staring at the marathoner and thinking they could never run a marathon.

One of my inspirations to running the marathon were the millions of people who have done it before.

People of all ages and sizes have run and made it. If they could do it, why couldn't I? I recently read about a guy in India who was one hundred and three and was still running marathons. Even more remarkable was the fact that he did not start running until his nineties. That is crazy, but true.

It goes to show it is never too late to start. While there may be many people simply incapable to do physically challenging feats like running a marathon, we are all capable (no matter what our age or circumstance) of making progress in the spiritual life. We just have to begin.

So how do we do that? There are lots of different ways. One of the most beautiful aspects of our faith is how unique it is. Catholic means universal and the fact that we are all bonded together as the Body of Christ is an awesome one. In addition to this common bond is our own personal relationship with Jesus. Because each of us is uniquely created by God and our life's circumstances and personalities are varied, so is our walk with the Lord. What works for one person may not be as effective for another.

In the fitness world, many people really like yoga. For others, they enjoy biking or running. Others like weight training. Engaging in a variety of exercises is the best approach to overall health and fitness.

However, within that, there are still things that seem to work for us better than others.

That is what you need to figure out for yourself. Let's take the Rosary as an example. This is one of the staples in the spiritual diet of many Catholics. As a private devotion, the Church does not require us to pray the Rosary. It is not on the same level as participating in Sunday Mass (as far as what the Church asks of us). However, it can still be extremely powerful in building up our faith.

The traditional method of praying the Rosary is to meditate upon the designated mysteries while you are reciting the various prayers. This has tremendous benefit as it assists us in reflecting upon what Jesus went through in dying for our sins. For me personally, I have found this way of praying the Rosary to be difficult. Perhaps I have a touch of spiritual ADD (Attention Deficit Disorder). Oftentimes, I get distracted and sidetracked to the point of diminished focus.

One technique that helps me is to physically get up and move around. I love walking and praying. In particular, being outside in nature is especially invigorating. There is something about God's creation that provides a divine backdrop for my quiet time with the Lord. The fresh air awakens my senses and the flow of blood to my brain helps keep me mentally sharp. One of my deepest spiritual states occurs when I am jogging and praying the Rosary at the same time.

Another tweak that I have found helpful is to personalize the Hail Mary prayers. Instead of reciting the last segment as "Holy Mary, Mother of God, pray for us sinners now and at the hour of our death," I will pray "Holy Mary, Mother of God, pray for Cindy, now and at the hour of her death." I sometimes alternate names each time or pray an entire decade or rosary with the intention of interceding for one person. This is another technique that helps me to stay focused.

With rote prayer, it is easy to end up mindlessly repeating words without being mentally or spiritually present. For many people, praying the Rosary the traditional way works just fine. I am just sharing the idea that you may want to experiment a little bit to find out what works best for you.

No matter what prayer style you choose, you still need to realistically assess your path. Sometimes, people go to a retreat or have some other profound encounter with the Lord and then want to jump into the deep end of the pool right away. The newfound zealousness may cause them to run too fast at the beginning of the race with the potential of them "hitting the wall" not long after. Our spiritual life is indeed a marathon and not a sprint. As the Holy

Spirit leads and empowers you to run faster, by all means, go for it.

The important part is to not get ahead of the Spirit where you are trying too hard to do your own thing without the promptings and guidance of the One who desires to bring you home to the finish line.

Examples of some spiritual warmup exercises

Going to a daily Mass during the week in addition to the Sunday Liturgy

Praying a decade of the Rosary each day the first week and then increasing that a decade each week until you are doing a full rosary

Reading a chapter of the Bible each night or once a week - I would suggest starting with the Gospel passages and also having a good Bible commentary that you read each passage with as well

Getting involved at an entry level in a parish ministry

Starting a journal to chronicle the movements within your spirit

Picking up a good spiritual book (besides this one of course ☺) and absorbing it in stages

Listening to a Catholic radio station on the way to work or doing the same with praise and worship music

Visiting the local nursing home and signing up to socialize with someone or stopping by a food pantry or homeless shelter and inquiring as to how you can assist that day

The main thing is to start with something, but to proceed slowly and with purpose. At the parish I work at, people will say we have ninety plus ministries. Not sure if that is entirely accurate as it seems to be a moving target, but one thing is for sure – we do have a lot to offer and to get involved with. Most parishes (especially larger ones) usually do. It can be overwhelming. How will you know where God is calling you and how you can use your gifts?

One answer is to take the Living Your Strengths (LYS) assessment. Outside the Church arena, this is also called Strengthsfinder. Many companies and organizations utilize this approach. It is a program and process that originated and is run by Gallup. Backed by years of solid research, this is an amazing tool that many have found to be very beneficial.

You begin by taking the Gallup online assessment which costs around $20. You answer random questions in quick succession and it takes about thirty to forty minutes to complete. Once done, it gives you your top five Signature Themes (out of a possible thirty-four). These Themes are your God given talents – personality traits and modes of operation that are more natural to you. Living Your Strengths is a book that has catholicized the concepts. The basic descriptions of each Theme are the same, but the book goes more in depth as to what those Themes mean for your faith and how you can develop them to be more effective in how you minister to others.

My own parish has been doing LYS for several years in different ways. Most of our parish leaders have taken the assessment along with many of our adult/teen parishioners. We offer one day seminars to help people process and make use of their Themes. For those that desire to go deeper, we have the Journey, which is a seven week course. In addition, we offer one on one individual LYS coaching. You do not need all of this for it to have value although the more you do with it, the more valuable it becomes.

Just taking the assessment and reading the descriptions can be affirming and life changing. As the title suggests, it is about living in your strengths. So often, we are hung up on trying to fix our weaknesses. This usually leads to discouragement and failure. The LYS process does just the opposite. It lifts our spirits as we discover the wonderful traits that God has blessed us with. A lot of adults have that "a-ha" moment where they say "Yes, I felt that way all my life – that is totally me!" It helps us to understand why we may do the things we do or act a certain way. It frees us from trying to be like other people and to be ourselves in a very authentic and liberating way.

This newfound self-awareness can help us as we discern what God may be calling us to or how to go about it. For example, one of the Gallup Themes is called Relator. This is a person who loves to relate to people one on one. They normally enjoy deep conversation. At a party, they are perfectly content to socialize with a handful of people all night long. This is what they are good at and are energized by.

Another Theme is called WOO (which stands for Winning Others Over). This is the kind of individual who likes to work the room and meet as many people as possible. They grow restless conversing with just a few people when there are so many to interact with.

In terms of our nursing home scenario, someone who has Relator as one of their top Themes may feel much more comfortable trying to set up and cultivate a couple of long term relationships with designated residents (visit the same people each time). The individual with WOO might be more energized by free lancing it and being able to stop by several rooms or perhaps they would want to look at the schedule and come when there are organized social activities involving lots of people at once. Do you see the difference?

If you might be called to assist in the parish youth ministry program and you have WOO, volunteering to prepare the meals in the kitchen could prove to be a source of frustration for you whereas you might be perfect to be the official greeter - to make sure everyone gets welcomed in a warm, friendly way. That is your sweet spot. That is what you do best. You are energized by it and you are good at it. This is what God has created you to do. This is how you serve best. Of course, there is nothing wrong with preparing food in the back or doing behind the scenes work. Many times, there are tasks to accomplish which may not always be life-giving, but they still need to be done and you are pitching in to help the cause or ease someone's burden.

I know people who really want to help the kids, but are terrified at the prospect of giving a talk or they feel uncomfortable socializing. They feel much better being in the back serving in those roles.

If you have Relator as your Theme, your strong suit might be as a small group leader that can help the kids go deeper in their relationship with Christ. You can start to see where knowing your gifts can be incredibly helpful in discerning how best to spend your time.

In the church world, I think many of us get caught up in the "empty spot, warm body" trap. We have some empty spots to fill. Warm bodies come forward (Catholic guilt does still exist) and we have our solution. Wrong. We have filled the immediate surface need, but have masked the problem. Just because someone has a pulse does not mean they are being called to serve in that capacity. As church administrators and staff, we can be just as guilty in all of this. It takes more time and effort to assist our volunteers in figuring out their gifts and how to use them than to simply slot them in. That is part of our human nature – to take the easy way out.

There is a better way. No, there is a <u>much</u> better way and the LYS process is a big part of that. Certainly, other personality profiles (like Myers-Briggs) have tremendous value as well. LYS is not the only show in town. The main thing is to do what you can to help you discover how you are wired, what you are called to do with those gifts and how you can develop and maximize them over the course of your lifetime.

Oftentimes, certain Themes are naturally grouped together. In other words, it is common for people with a certain Theme to have another one that is connected with it in their top five. Input and Learner are two of these. A person who has Input enjoys collecting various things – this can include information and ideas. A person who has Learner enjoys the process of learning new things. You can see where these two Themes can be closely connected. When people share their top five with me, it is very common for me to hear them say Input and Learner. One of the reasons I hear this might be because those are my own top two Themes.

For me (and others like me) who has both of these Themes, I love to research. The internet is an Input-Learner's absolute dream. It is like having the world's library at your fingertips. Like anything else, this can be good or bad. The shadow side could be an addiction to watching YouTube videos all day or surfing the Web endlessly and without purpose. It could be the ultimate time waster for many of us. We have to guard against things like that.

On the flip side, we could put that researching to good use. We have a woman on our LYS team at our parish who also is an Input-Learner. She loves to research and is great at it. She is continually going to various websites to find out the latest trends in helping us to become more effective in our ministry efforts. It is not uncommon for her to be forwarding another enlightening article or video that she found online. For many people for whom Input-Learner may be far down their list of thirty-four, researching like this could be draining – a necessary evil at times. For people like her (and me), it is a labor of love.

You can see how living in your strengths can be so powerful and effective for you and those around you. That is why this is a critical step in the warming up period. Before you get too far down the road in working out, it is essential to know yourself so as to come up with the best game plan possible.

6 STRENGTH TRAINING FOR YOUR SOUL

As I mentioned earlier, I was a pretty active kid growing up. I was never a star athlete and did not have exceptional skills in any one sport. I was a Jack of all sports – decent in most, but a master of none. With graduation, my official athletic career was done (at least in terms of organized team sports). I still desired to stay in shape so I joined the campus gym my freshman year of college. It was a small facility with a smattering of various cardio and strength training equipment. The college students who came were pretty casual with their workouts and the atmosphere was more conducive to finding a date than actual physical fitness.

Knowing very little about how to build and maintain muscle, I came up with a simple, comfortable routine. There were about three to four exercises that I enjoyed and would do every time I went in. I would do three sets of ten repetitions for each of them with usually the same weight each time. I would do a set, rest a while and then move on to the next set. This was my routine three days a week. It was safe, easy and predictable.

During this first semester of college, I developed a strong friendship with a guy across the hall from me. Ryan also had an interest in working out and would do so faithfully. His dad was a bodybuilder and was still competing in competitions in his mid-forties. Ryan and I got to talking one day and he asked me about my workout routine. I explained what I did and he asked if I wanted to join him at his gym to try it out. Maybe we could work out together. He had been wanting a workout partner. It sounded good to me. It was worth checking out.

The next day after class, I walked up to Ryan's place. The Body Shop was a privately run gym a few blocks off campus. You entered the building at street level and immediately hiked up this long set of stairs to the second floor. With every step, the temperature got noticeably warmer. As I ascended to the top landing, I felt like I had entered a different world. The air was thick with sweat. With the heat and humidity, it felt like a tropical rain forest. Heavy metal music pulsated through my body as it rang out through the speakers hanging from the ceiling. There were only a couple of females and they did not appear interested in meeting anybody new. Regardless of the gender, everyone had an intense demeanor about them. Several of the guys looked like they could double for Arnold Schwarzenegger (who at the time was still held up as the bodybuilding icon). This place was hard core.

My friend Ryan was even more intense in how he did his workout routine. With an enthusiastic grin, he said "Just follow my lead." After warming up for quite some time, I was thinking we were maybe halfway done. Oh no. We had just begun.

Ryan jumped quickly from one exercise to another. We would flip between two or three different pieces of equipment only to then jump to entirely new exercises. Not only were there lots of sets and repetitions for each one, we never seemed to rest in between. He explained that we could get a good cardiovascular workout this way as well by keeping our heart rate up the whole time. I could barely catch my breath before I was hoisting some other heavy weight. I put on a brave face, but my body was in shock. This was nothing like what I was used to. It took every ounce of energy just to try and keep up. We kept going - lifting heavier and heavier weight.

After what seemed like an eternity, Ryan finally announced "That is probably enough for one day." That was the understatement of the year. That was enough for one semester. My body was reeling as I stumbled down the long stairway to the exit. My legs were so shaky that I felt as though they were going to give way and I was going to helplessly fall to my death. By the grace of God, I was able to make it to the bottom and somehow push open the door.

When I stepped outside, I collapsed on to the nearby grassy area where I thought I was going to throw up. As I knelt down waiting for the heaving to begin, Ryan was asking me what I thought. What did I think??? I thought that I was going to die – that is what I thought. I thought this was absolute insanity. I thought this would be my last day of working out with Ryan at that horror house they called a gym. My easy, comfortable routine at the campus facility worked just fine. Why would I choose to do this again? I thought thanks, but no thanks Ryan. This will be my one and only time doing this.

When I got home, the fatigue and pain were in full force and when I woke up the next day, every muscle in my body announced its presence. For the next couple of days, I was far too sore to do any working out, but I did have plenty of time to contemplate my experience. Ryan was encouraging me to go back with him and to give it another try. The slogan "no pain, no gain" kept going through my mind. I certainly had plenty of pain and I did desire the gain of muscle mass. I knew I was in a rut with my old routine. It was not doing anything for me anymore.

Deep down, I yearned for more. Amazingly, I told Ryan I would give him a week. What he did, I would do.

We returned to the place of pain and I resolved to stick with it for seven days no matter what. It was tough again, but with each passing day, it did get easier. My body got stronger. My endurance levels went up. I could feel myself developing and evolving into the person I wanted to be. From that moment on, I was hooked. Not only did I continue with working out with my friend and being a member of that gym, I have continued to exercise in the same, intense fashion in the thirty years since that time.

I learned a great deal from Ryan and his dad about fitness and nutrition. This helped to lay a foundation within me that has continued on to this day. I have since passed this information and practice on to many others along the way including my own family.

The goal of strength training is to build muscle, get stronger and achieve or maintain a high level of fitness. In order to do this effectively, you must continually challenge yourself in new ways. Our muscles adapt to whatever we are doing. Many people mistakenly believe that our muscles grow when we are lifting weights. We are actually doing the opposite. Heavy, strenuous lifting tears the muscle fibers down. This triggers a response within your body. It basically says "Gosh, if we have to lift heavy weight like this, we better develop more muscle fiber so we are better prepared next time." While you sleep, your amazing God given body goes into high gear, not only repairing muscle cells, but building more and that is how you get bigger and stronger. The more that you stress and challenge the body, the more it adapts and responds positively.

This is accomplished several ways, but the key is to mix things up. You need to change the types of exercises, the order of them, the amount of weight being used, the timing of them, etc. In other words, you keep your body guessing. You need to alter your routine periodically to keep it fresh and to keep growing.

Similarly, we can get into our spiritual ruts and routines. If you want a deeper, more profound experience of the Holy Spirit, you are going to have to challenge yourself in new ways. Opening your mind and heart in new ways allows God to work His grace more completely within you.

A staple of almost every Confirmation program is the weekend retreat. Parents will sometimes ask if their teen really has to go and if so, why do we require it? I have always been one to make it mandatory (allowing for reasonable exceptions of course). I have done so not to put hurdles on their path to receiving the

Sacrament or to give them the illusion that they must somehow earn Confirmation. Nothing can be further from the truth. Ultimately, it is a gift of grace that is freely given by our Creator. No, we bring kids on a retreat because it can be a spiritual game changer for them. So what is so special about the retreat? Let's dive a little deeper to find out.

Let me qualify my statements up front by stating someone could become an absolute saint here on Earth without ever having gone on a retreat. There is nothing magical about retreats per se. What? But you just said it was a spiritual game changer. Yes, it can be. However, it has nothing to do with a certain retreat or retreats in general.

I always tell kids that there is no more God out at the retreat center in the woods than there is back in their own homes. God remains present always and everywhere. By virtue of their baptism, the Holy Spirit dwells within them. God is not different on retreat. We are. How so? Because we get away from our normal routine. Because we are out of our comfort zone. Because we free ourselves from everyday distractions. Because we are usually experiencing God's wondrous creation. Because we have begun to let our guard down. Because we are focused on hearing God's voice. Because we devote significant time to prayer and reflection. Because we are surrounded by a loving and supportive community that inspires us in our faith. Because we receive the Sacraments of Reconciliation and Eucharist. All of these things open our hearts and minds to God's movement in our lives. It is that openness that makes all the difference. A retreat is a great vehicle to make that happen.

As we know, retreats are not just for kids anymore. There are lots of fantastic retreat experiences for adults offered by parishes or diocesan entities. In addition, there are retreat experiences offered in various regions. Most of them are centered in community and rich in fellowship. Some are solitary in nature.

Many years ago, I was doing a graduate project for my pastoral ministry degree. Part of my work involved filming some scenes at a hermitage called Pacem in Terris located in central Minnesota. The title of my project was from Psalm 46:11 "Be still and know that I am God." This retreat center epitomized that concept. Everything about the center pointed to that one reality. It was a perfect backdrop for my message. While there, the director was very gracious and insisted that I come back as a hermit myself instead of a film maker. I explained that I did not really think a silent retreat was my style and besides I was too busy with a full-time job and going to graduate school full-time. To her credit, she persisted in encouraging me to make the time. Her words stuck and I felt convicted by the Holy Spirit to indeed make the effort. I cleared my calendar a couple of months later and made the pilgrimage out to the retreat center.

Pacem in Terris is Latin for Peace on Earth and this place really was. It was nestled in a beautifully wooded forest with lots of privacy. As soon as you stepped out of the car, you knew you were somewhere special. It was so quiet and tranquil. After giving me a warm hug and friendly welcome, Shirley showed me to my cabin. It was very simple with just the basics. There was no TV, phone or electronics. Instead, you were treated with a giant picture window that allowed you to gaze upon God's creation. Everything contributed to a relaxed, focused environment.

When I had booked my retreat, Shirley insisted that I stay at least two nights. One night was never enough. She said it usually took one whole day and night just to let go of the worldly anxieties and to physically rest. Part of the experience is to fast on bread and water most of the day and then hermits are welcome to join the staff for a communal dinner each evening. That is the only time talking is allowed.

I unpacked my things and sat on the bed unsure of what to do. I was so accustomed to running around and adhering to a schedule that I found myself a little lost. I did end up sleeping and sleeping and sleeping some more. Shirley was right. I was like everyone else and had come physically and mentally exhausted from the kind of lifestyle that we were accustomed to. I woke up in the morning completely refreshed and ready for my God moments.

After a great day of Bible reading, prayer and introspection, I was treated to a special surprise. God had blessed us with a snowstorm that evening. With my candle burning on my bed stand, I was mesmerized by the beauty of the snowflakes that were rapidly coming down outside my picture window. Growing up in northern Minnesota, I had experienced lots of snowstorms before, but I never really spent much time getting caught up in them. I might glance out the window to see it was snowing and then go back to watching my movie. In this instance, I had no other distractions. I was a captive audience. What a stunning sight to behold. I eventually drifted off feeling as though I had died and gone to heaven.

I awoke to a bright light pouring through my picture window. The storm had passed, the clouds had parted and in its place was a full moon shining in all of its glory. I decided it was a great time to go for a midnight walk. As the new fallen snow quietly crunched below my boots, I made my way down to a dock that overlooked a lake. It was the perfect peaceful setting. Sacred silence at its best. It felt as though time stood still and heaven itself had opened up. That moment was the ultimate cherry on top of a spiritual sundae that I will never forget. Psalm 46:11 was being played out before my eyes.

Of course that is just one retreat place and one retreat experience. There are so many out there to explore and edify our souls. I propose going on an adult retreat as not only one of our first steps, but as an ongoing part of our spiritual routine.

In addition to a retreat, what else can you do to stretch your soul? There are a myriad of ways to open yourself up to God's grace and wisdom. What you will actually do depends largely on your discernment of your gifts and how God can touch and transform you personally. The spiritual journey can be very unique to each one of us. Besides frequent reception of the Sacraments (Reconciliation and Eucharist) which I have alluded to already, I would like to offer a few concrete ideas (exercises if you will) to get you thinking and to form a spiritual workout routine.

Devotional Discipline

In the spirit of Psalm 46:11, we need to be still on a regular basis. This is where the concept of quiet time comes in. It is critical to set aside time each day to spend in prayer and reflection. We will never hear God's voice or grow in His grace if we are always on the run. It is helpful to most people to create a routine where we have our quiet time in the same place at the same time each day. This sacred space should be free from distractions – no TV, radio, internet, phone, etc. Also, you should be well rested, but not sleepy. I can speak to many well-intentioned "pillow prayers" in my own life. Get too comfortable and you will find yourself waking up minutes or hours later wondering what happened.

What you do during your quiet time is up to you. It could be a combination of things like praying the Rosary, reading Scripture, praying the Liturgy of the Hours, meditating in silence, interceding for a list of people and intentions or going to daily Mass. In the movie War Room, the main character makes an ordinary space in her residence one of supernatural significance. She retreats to this sacred space to intercede for the world. Create your own war room by establishing a time, place and routine where you consistently connect with the Creator of the cosmos.

Bible Basics

When it comes to reading the Bible, this can feel like a foreign land for Catholics. Many of us do not feel educated enough or comfortable enough to crack open the Scriptures. We have relied on the Church to do the reading for us when we hear the Word of God proclaimed at Mass. Because of this, our Bibles tend to collect dust and act more like furniture than faith builders. This has to change if we want to have the mind of God. People think God does not speak to them because they do not hear His voice. Turns out God has spoken and revealed a lot to us already. How many words are there in the Bible? The short answer is a lot. Think of all the wisdom and inspiration we are missing out on. So where do we begin and how do we proceed?

Just like in other aspects, there is no one way to use or read the Scriptures. Allow me to touch on one method that I have found to be very fruitful.

Lectio Divina (Latin for Divine Reading) is an ancient practice of praying with the Scriptures. The key word here is praying. This is not simply reading the passage to understand its meaning or to figure out how the story develops. This is not a merely academic exercise. No, this is engaging with the Word of God in a transformative way. There are variations in this practice as well.

Begin by selecting a passage that you feel drawn toward. Most of the Psalms are well suited for this purpose, but it can be any section of the Bible. Read the words slowly and purposefully. Take a minute to let them soak in. Then come back to the passage and read it even more methodically. Again, this is not to analyze, critique or study. You do not want to project your own thoughts and ideas on to the page. Instead, you are opening your mind and heart to what the Holy Spirit wants to reveal to you. After a second reading and prayerful contemplation, you would repeat the process one more time. After you are done, you just sit with the text. You are in a divine dialogue with the Lord except that you want to be the one doing most of the listening. What word or phrase seemed to resonate within you? What message or idea keeps coming back up? Where do you sense God's guidance, challenge or comfort in this moment?

Be careful not to select too long of a passage or try to do a whole chapter in one sitting. Less is more as you are diving deep. Each word could be tremendously powerful. Allow God's grace to move freely within your mind and soul. As you receive His wisdom and comfort, be sure to spend time thanking Him and asking Him to show you where to make corrections in your life. It could mean a shift in your attitudes, actions or disposition. At other times, it is confirmation that you are on the right track. In other instances, God may be calling you to intercede for specific people or situations.

Lectio Divina is an adventure every time you enter into it. You never know what God has in store for you. Our Lord is full of surprise and intrigue. To be able to commune with the Creator of the cosmos in such an intimate and personal way is something that everyone should do as often as possible. The beautiful aspect of this type of praying is that it can be done anywhere at any time as long as you have the Word of God available to you.

Catechetical Cardio

Having spent my entire professional ministry career in faith formation, catechesis is, of course, near and dear to my heart. However, I want to repeat the one important distinction. Just knowing about God is not enough. Memorizing facts and developing deep insight means nothing unless that head knowledge makes it to the heart and hands as well.

Having said that, we absolutely need to be learning more and more about our faith all the time if we are to make spiritual progress. One way to do this is to sign up for a class or Bible study at your parish. The benefit of this is that you get to hear insights and wisdom that others have to offer whether it be the instructor or participants. If your own parish does not offer much, you can see what surrounding parishes may have or what your diocese has scheduled. If you are like many adults, you might feel intimidated to go to a class or Bible study because you might look stupid or naïve. The others will be full of theological insight and you barely remember how to look things up. I can assure you that this fear is completely unfounded. Yes, many people there are well versed in biblical matters, but they are equally thrilled that you would grace them with your presence. Every group leader or member that I have ever met is ecstatic to see new faces and hear fresh perspectives. Don't ever let fear hold you back.

There are tons of excellent books out on the market that can assist you in understanding the faith at a deeper level. You just need to be careful as to the source and legitimacy of the information. This is especially true when it comes to Church teachings. If your book involves doctrinal statements of faith and morals, then it should have an Imprimatur on the inside cover. If it is more spiritually based (like this one), then it normally would not have one. You want to make sure you are learning what the Church actually professes and holds to be true instead of what someone thinks the Church teaches. Just make sure you are drawing from trusted, reputable Catholic sources.

Of course, the Catechism of the Catholic Church is the number one destination when it comes to Church teaching. This is our best resource to clarify various dogmas and doctrines and should be consulted whenever a question arises.

In addition to books, there are many audio CDs and videos that explain the faith in a very beautiful way. Our parish purchases CDs from Augustine Institute and makes them available in the narthex of our church. I know many parishioners who listen to these on their way to work (particularly if they have long commutes).

As I mentioned before, the internet is like having the world's library at your fingertips – what an awesome tool it is. You could spend days on end watching YouTube videos or surfing various websites or blogs. An infinite amount of great information abounds with the usual cautionary disclaimer of being mindful of all the misinformation that exists as well. Internet videos or blogs do not come with Imprimaturs so you need to be extra aware of what you are taking in and the credibility that it comes with.

There are three websites that I recommend. The first is the official US Bishops website at www.usccb.org. This is a good source for Church documents. Catholic.com is the website for Catholic Answers, an apologetics ministry based out of San Diego. The name says it all – they provide orthodox answers regarding Church teaching and explain the differences with other Protestant denominations as well as other world religions. Since I have been involved in youth ministry all these years, Lifeteen.com has been a go to site for many of our young people. Life teen runs a cutting edge ministry that produces content not only good for teens, but adults of all ages. I would also suggest checking out the Fr. Mike Schmitz videos on YouTube. He has a phenomenal way of explaining difficult concepts.

One of the programs that our parish recently purchased is the online subscription called Formed. It contains several videos like Bishop Barron's Catholicism series or the Symbolon program featuring top notch national speakers on location in Rome explaining the faith in an inspirational and informative manner. You can stream them to your laptop anytime, anywhere on your schedule.

There are many apps for your phone that are useful and convenient in the prayer life. The one I use most is Laudette which has the readings for that day, Liturgy of the Hours, saints and so much more.

From the early Church Fathers to recent Papal Encyclicals, there is so much to learn with over 2,000 years of Church understanding. Catechesis is not just for kids anymore. In fact, it was never meant to be.

For some reason, many Catholics got the false notion that we were all done learning when we got confirmed as if Confirmation meant graduation from the Church. Nothing could be further from the truth. It is just the opposite. As a Sacrament of Initiation, Confirmation is just a beginning, not an ending. Learning and growing in our faith is a life-long endeavor. There is nothing better than learning things at an adult level. That is why catechesis should be a staple in our spiritual workout routine.

Marian Movement

Growing up, I never prayed the Rosary and my family never referenced Mary at all. She was just simply the mother of Jesus and the only time I ever thought about her was when I saw her in the manger scene and sang about her in a Christmas song. That all changed my sophomore year of college.

I was actively involved in the Newman Center at our university. The Center ran what was called the Newman Club. This was basically youth group for college students. We were a very small contingent of young adults who gathered at the rectory with the pastor to discuss various elements of the faith and how they intersected with our daily lives.

One evening, Theresa, who was my same age, was facilitating the conversation. The topic was Marian apparitions. In particular, she focused on the events taking place in Medjugorje, Yugoslavia. She explained that Mary was apparently appearing to some teens on a regular basis in this small, mountain village and it had become a popular site. Faithful pilgrims were streaming in from all over the world and there were reports of many miracles taking place – the biggest of which was spiritual in nature with thousands being reignited in their walk with God.

As Theresa went into more and more detail, I became enamored with the entire story. Theresa and I walked back to the dorms together that night and she was saying how she wished she could experience a miracle of her own. There were several reports of people who saw the sun spinning or their rosaries would turn color. I told her to stay open and to keep praying. You never know when God would surprise her with something miraculous.

The very next day, Theresa called all excited. Her rosary (which she had passed around the circle the night before) had indeed turned color overnight. What I mean by this is that certain links (not the beads themselves) had turned a gold color. Not all of them. Only the ones that linked the Our Father bead for each decade. The previous night she explained this very phenomenon and I remember carefully examining her rosary – her links were all silver that night. When Theresa showed me her rosary now, I could see the links that were now gold in color. Being more skeptical in nature, I held them up to the light to examine them in detail. Even if Theresa had tried to perpetrate a hoax (which she would not do as she was one of the most honest, faith filled people I knew), I do not see how she could have pulled this off by having some of the links turn gold while all the others remained silver.

The whole experience piqued my curiosity and I began digging deeper into this Medjugorje phenomenon. I started reading newsletters written by a Lutheran named Wayne Weible. His own personal story was a fascinating one and too much to go into here. Suffice it to say that his story (and subsequent books) had a profound effect on my understanding and appreciation of Mary.

My son, who is about to enter his third year of seminary, feels called to the priesthood. He attributes much of his discernment to the intercession of Mary. In particular, there have been many "coincidences" of Our Lady of Guadalupe popping up and seemingly guiding him down this vocational path.

Particular devotions to Mary or any of the other saints are completely optional. However, who would not want to employ an army in heaven to be interceding for you? At a bare minimum, I would suggest you at least ask your Confirmation/patron saint to pray for you.

Giving Growth

When I work with parents, I will pose the same statement and universally, they will always finish the sentence in the same way. Parents will say, "I do not care what my kid wants to do in life or where they want to go as long as they are happy." We all have the same basic goal for our kids as well for ourselves

– to be happy. I have adjusted that saying for myself proclaiming that "I do not care what my kids do in life or where they go as long as they are *holy*." I do not say this to be overly pious or religious. I say this because holiness leads to happiness – true happiness.

Earthy or worldly happiness is only temporary. If our team wins, we are happy, but only for a little while. Same goes for any other circumstance in our life. If we get accepted into a certain college or get a promotion at work or win a door prize at the charity event, we are happy. That is until the next set of circumstances hits us and as we all know, not everything in life goes well. Our journey is filled with ups and downs. Our happiness should never be dependent upon the circumstances of our life and yet that is how most people tend to live. "How are you doing?" is the standard greeting and the response (whether verbalized or not) largely depends on the circumstances of that particular day.

Wouldn't it be great if we could be freed from the bondages of everyday events? To live a life filled with joy, purpose, passion and meaning? We can and should. That is what the faith life is all about. The more that we fill our lives up with Christ, the more that we will have His eternal perspective. That is where we will discover true joy and fulfillment.

One of the best ways to experience this is to live a life of generosity. Do this simple exercise with me. After you read these instructions, I want you to do the following. Set down your book and extend both of your arms out in front of you with your palms up. Then I want you to clench both of your fists as tight as you can (really tight) and hold them that way for one whole minute. Do not let up – you should feel the burn. After the minute is up, go ahead and release. Do this activity now.

How did that feel? Society has conditioned us to believe that the goal in life is to grab on to as much as we possibly can, hold on as tight as we can for as long as we can. This consumeristic, materialistic mindset is somehow supposed to bring us happiness. I do not know about you, but when I do that, I feel stress, tension and anxiety. Conversely, when we let go and open up our hands, we feel so much better. This is what we were made for – to give and to serve.

I never had the privilege of meeting Mother Teresa. However, I have read many articles and testimonies from people who have. One thing always seems to stand out when people describe their interactions with her and that was her overflowing joy. At first, this struck me as odd. Here is a woman who has devoted her entire life to serving the poorest of the poor. She has given up everything to pick up dying bodies off the street of Calcutta, to care for their wounds and to provide them some measure of comfort and dignity. I can see where people would greatly admire and respect her for her sacrificial nature – where they would commend her for her dedication, hard work, loyalty and determination. But joy? In worldly standards, what she did would be anything but joyful. Exemplary yes, but joyful? Therein lies the secret of true happiness. The more we give, the happier we become. Dying to self is just what the Divine Physician ordered.

We used to bring kids on a mission trip to a Catholic orphanage called Nuestros Pequenos Hermanos (meaning Our Little Brothers and Sisters). The organization (NPH) continues to do extraordinary work and operates several orphanages throughout Latin America.

The one we went to was located about an hour outside the capital city of Tegucigalpa, Honduras. They housed approximately six hundred orphans from toddlers to high school age. They lived on a ranch up in the mountains. It was very picturesque and peaceful. Compared to life on the streets, being in the orphanage was quite nice. Even though the kids came from broken homes in which their parents died or were simply unable to take care of them, NPH did their best to create that family environment. In fact, well-meaning donors would inquire about the possibility of adopting some of the kids only to be denied because the orphanage had a philosophy of family. They wanted to let the kids know that once they joined NPH, they would never be adopted out. Even though they had experienced severe trauma and instability before, NPH would now become that place of unconditional love and acceptance where they would forever be part of their family. This message of love was cloaked in very practical ways as the kids received three meals a day, shelter, schooling, spiritual formation, medical and dental treatments, vocational training, etc.

As wonderful as all of this was, it was still a very simple life in comparison to what our kids were accustomed to. In fact, when we would process the day's events with our teens, I would hear the same sentiments. They felt so sorry for these kids who had so little. The orphans lived in dormitory style buildings and all of their belongings (their shoes, clothes, books, and personal products) had to fit in one school locker which meant they did not have very much at all. Again, our kids would see this and feel so sorry for the orphans. No phones, X-Box, internet, computers or cable TV for them.

An interesting development would take place during our visit there. By the time our seven or ten day trip was done, all of our teens were doing a 180. They would be asking themselves a different question "How can these kids be so happy when they have so little?" I would then reply, "Maybe it is because they have so little, that they are so happy." They were not caught up in consumerism and materialism like we were. They were free to live, love, play and give. And give they did.

One of the striking examples of this related to food. While they received three meals a day, there was not much variation in these meals. By necessity, there was lots of beans and rice each meal every day. Sprinkle in some tortillas and chicken and that was about the extent of variety that we experienced when we were there. There was at least one exception to this.

Every month, all of the kids that were celebrating their birthday would be loaded up on the bus for a trip to the capital city. It was there that they got to go to Pizza Hut. What is a very normal staple for us to consume was an absolute rare treat for them. They were allowed to get three pieces of pizza. So what did they do? Many of them would eat one piece and then carefully wrap up the other two pieces in a napkin. They would then place them in their backpack, bring them all the way back to the orphanage and share with their fellow brothers and sisters. Can you imagine? I kept thinking how hungry I would be and how I would inhale that pizza in an instant. Not them. They operated in a different spirit – one which was defined by generosity and love. That is why they were so happy.

This idea of dying to self is indeed a stretch for us. We have been conditioned for so long to think first of our own wants, needs and desires. We have been brainwashed to think that bigger is better and the more we buy and consume, the better off we will be. If we are honest, most of us have bought into this lie to some degree or another. I know it has been a struggle for me. Perhaps it has been for you too.

The good news is that there is hope. This is a relatively simple fix. Not necessarily easy, but simple. Stewardship is typically categorized into three areas of our life – time, talent and treasure. Let's take a peek at each of these to see where we can grow.

Stewardship of Time

God has blessed us with twenty-four hours today and then if we are fortunate enough, another twenty-four hours tomorrow and the day after that. Every hour, every minute is a gift. The key question is how are we going to spend that time? There is no doubt that most of us feel overloaded and that there is never enough time to do what we want to do.

Think back to yesterday and try to sketch out all the things you did over the course of the day – assign approximate times to these activities. Do the same thing (in a more general way) for this past week.

Are you maximizing your time? Are you doing things efficiently? Do you have too many commitments? Do you need to simplify or let go of certain areas in your life? Is your day filled with Earthly pursuits? How much quality time have you spent with God? Have you been actively seeking ways to serve others? Are you striking a healthy balance so you can get adequate rest, nutrition and exercise?

If you only had a week to live, how would you spend that week differently? Are your core values being honored and prioritized with the way you are spending your time?

Naturally, there are various obligations that we have to meet and there are many moments out of our control. Very few of us have the luxury of meditating on top of a mountain all day long. We have jobs, families, bills, schoolwork, etc. However, even within those times, there are probably moments that we can seize to live out our calling more fully.

For example, think of all the time that many of us spend commuting to work. Instead of listening to talk radio or a play by play of the game or any general music station, I encourage you to look at spiritual alternatives.

All major markets have Catholic or other Christian radio stations. Several people listen to audio CDs by top Catholic speakers. Or my personal favorite is to turn everything off and simply pray. Traffic jams are a struggle for me as I feel so helpless just sitting and waiting (and feeling like I am wasting so much time). I have tried (not always successfully ☺) to turn that around by thanking God for this extra time to spend with Him. Oftentimes, I will pray for the people in the vehicles around me or for the people involved in the car accident up ahead. These are opportunities to spend with our Creator. Traffic jams can really be traffic blessings if we look at them in this whole new way.

If you take mass transit, bring a spiritual book to read or do some Bible reflections. I live close enough to work to where I can bike when it is nice enough outside. It is fifteen minutes of pure peace and bliss. People will oftentimes comment on how admirable it is that I bike because I am getting a workout. When I bike, it is very casual so it is hardly a workout. I do not bike to work for exercise. I do it because it is good for the environment and I desire to live simply and with purpose. That joy ride to and from work is thirty minutes of clearing my head and reconnecting with my Lord. It is a win-win all the way around. At my last parish, I lived only six blocks from work and so I would walk each day. It was even better than biking as it forced me to slow down and to drink life in.

We all take showers or baths each day. This is another window to regularly connect with the Lord. Whether it be through singing or just plain conversation, start each day by offering it up to God.

If we were secretly recorded, I bet we would discover how much time is frittered away on superficial pursuits. This could include Web surfing, watching TV shows or following sports. Of course, there is nothing wrong or sinful about a reasonable amount of leisure or entertainment. We all need a mental break from the heaviness of life's demands. However, leisurely moments can easily digress into more of a slothful rut – wasting precious time and opportunity that could be spent in more noble pursuits.

One of my Earthly interests revolves around professional football. The NFL is the only sport that I follow with any commitment or interest. That is the good part. The bad part is that I have been overly consumed with it at times. This addiction was fueled by the internet explosion. Like anything else, if you want to know more and consume additional (often unnecessary) information, then the internet is your best friend and worst enemy. Not only would I watch the games on Sunday, but I would spend an inordinate amount of time looking up various websites to find the latest news on injuries, weather forecast and analyst predictions. When it was all said and done, the outcome of the game was still going to be the same regardless. All this really accomplished was two things. The first was an absolute misuse of

the time God had given me and the second was my
emotional investment in something that by all
accounts was quite trivial. Therefore, when my team
would eventually lose or get knocked out of the
playoffs, I would be devastated because I poured
some much of myself into the game. This was without
ever indulging in fantasy football which usually adds
a whole new layer to the obsession.

After realizing my addiction, I cut back substantially
where I do not bother going to websites and listening
in to see what the coach thought afterward. In
addition, I found it to be much less stressful to simply
record the game. Then I can skip through
commercials and all other slow moving phases to get
to the more interesting aspects of the contest. This
new approach not only saves a lot of time, but it helps
me keep the sport in its proper perspective. How we
steward our time is extremely important.

Stewardship of Talent

What we do with our God given talents is just as
important. Each one of us is incredibly unique. There
has never been anyone exactly like you in the history
of the world nor will there ever be. God has placed
you in a particular time, born to a specific family and
has graced you with a job, neighbors and
opportunities. You are called to be His hands and
feet. There may be a classmate or co-worker in your

life at this moment that only you can touch. Take a look around you. Be aware. Be alert. Ask the Holy Spirit to use you as His vessel of grace.

When it comes to talents, I think most of us have been discouraged enough to ignore them. We watch musical contestants on reality TV shows or professional athletes and we proclaim them as having real talent. They do indeed have incredible talent, but that is not to say that we are any less talented in things that matter. Being able to throw a football is nice, but what about having the patience and wisdom to counsel someone who just lost a family member? What about being that stable friend who is present day in and day out to encourage and support other people? What about tutoring disadvantaged kids so they finally feel like they have some real hope of a decent future?

Do an inventory of the talents and gifts that you have to offer. If you have trouble thinking of many, ask people that know and love you. They may see qualities in you that you are blinded to altogether.

My own talent in athletics is representative of most of my life. Growing up, I dreamed up being the next NBA or NFL star. Not only was this not anywhere in my future, but I was not even a star in college, high school, junior high or elementary school. In the small town I grew up in, I did get to play and even start on most of the teams, but that was only because there were so few players to choose from. Had I gone to a big school, I would have ridden the bench if I even made the team. I was decent at almost everything I did, but never spectacular. I wanted to excel in something, but never did. I could hold my own and help the team, but never stood out in any remarkable way. Everything for me was mostly average. On a good day, maybe I ascended to above average. As they describe college recruits, my floor was fairly high, but my ceiling was low. No matter how hard I tried, I was never going to be a star.

By the time I was in junior high, there was a local boy who was living my dream. His name was Kevin McHale – you may have heard of him. World champion forward for the famed Boston Celtics of the Larry Bird era. Kevin grew up in a town forty miles from where I lived. I remember reading a story about him and how he simply went up to the high school gym and would spend hours practicing his craft. You got the sense that all it took was hard work and determination. I thought, if he could do it, why not me? In between my 7th and 8th grade years, I would bike up to my local high school and spend countless hours perfecting my jump shot. Well, you know how this ends – in mediocrity. Why? For starters, Kevin was a foot taller than me. That always helps when playing professional basketball. On top of this, I did not have the eye/hand coordination nor the right touch in shooting nor the physical stamina to play at high levels. I could have shot baskets until I was blue in the face – I was never going to make it to the NBA no matter how hard I tried. This is where we have bought into a myth in our society.

We are told that we can be anything we want as long as we set our mind to it. This is incorrect. We are setting our kids up for failure when we tell them this. The mind and the will are very powerful forces. There is no doubt about this and I believe in fulfilling our highest potential. However, we need to assess our gifts and what God has crafted us to be. Striving to be an NBA star when God never intended me to be one is an exercise in futility. The sooner we accept some of these realities, the better off we will be. Why? Because it then frees us to cultivate the gifts that God did give us. If we spend our lives wishing or hoping to be someone else, we will never fulfill our own calling. And if we do not do so, who will? Assess your own individual gifts and see how you can develop and maximize them to serve others.

Stewardship of Treasure

One of the great myths about stewardship is that it is all about money. The second biggest myth is that it is not about money at all. As an overcorrection to the first misunderstanding, I hear this come out of the mouth of many well-meaning Catholics. I think Jesus would have something to say about that.

The Bible is filled with passages regarding our stewardship of treasure. Jesus touched on the topic of money and possessions more than his teachings on heaven and hell combined. Why so much emphasis on this? It is because this can be our biggest stumbling block in the spiritual life. Out of greed, selfishness, insecurity and fear, we cling to our financial treasure. Whether we crave financial prosperity or financial security, it can have a death grip on us and we don't even realize it. You hear the expression all the time. Money doesn't buy happiness. Most of us say this, but I am not sure we really believe it based upon our attitudes and actions. I say this not out of some high and lofty moral superiority. No, this comes from someone who has been mired in the same struggle that most of you have been. Ponder these questions.

If you lost your job today, would you be just as happy tomorrow?

Would you take it in stride if your stock portfolio took a big hit?

Do you find yourself yearning for just a little more money all the time?

How would you honestly feel if God asked you to give all you had to the poor?

If you are like me, these scenarios are incredibly tough and challenging. It is one thing to pray for someone or to volunteer for a couple of hours. It is quite another when you are asked to voluntarily relinquish the very thing that you have been striving for so long. That society has conditioned you to think is the ultimate prize. To let go of the fortress that you have put your trust and security in. To sacrifice that which brings your pleasure and comfort.

It is for these very reasons that we MUST be good stewards of our treasure. Our obsession with money is preventing us from living our lives in Christ. I always tell people that stewardship is not about the Church's need for money (although there are legitimate needs for this). It is about our need to give. It is good for us.

Imagine that your toddler has a playdate with the neighbor kids coming over. You are having coffee with some of the parents and right around the corner the children are playing with toys in the game room. Everything is going well until you hear your child scream "No, that's mine. You can't play with that." What would you do? If you are like most responsible parents, you would go in and tell your child to share. Not only because it is the right and polite thing to do, but because deep down you do not want your child to become a spoiled, rotten brat. When they share, it is not only good for the other children; it is good for your child. Their human nature is driving them to compete and be selfish with the toys. They need to learn to be kind, compassionate and loving. This is where we come in as parents. That is why sharing is so important.

Our Heavenly Father is looking down on us and saying "SHARE." Not only is it good for the poor and vulnerable, but it is good for us. It helps release us from the bondages of materialism. It allows God's grace to transform our hearts and minds to be more like Christ. We indeed become the very best versions of ourself.

How much should we share? There is no giving chart that factors in all of the variables that matter. Of course there are guidelines that can help us discern what God is asking of us. One of them most cited is the tithing principle found within the Old Testament. Tithing is an English term meaning tenth. God has asked us to give of our first fruits. The tithing principal mandates that we give ten percent of our income. This, by the way, is considered the minimum. If we are able to give more, we probably should. Jesus went further in his teachings and parables. One that comes to mind is the poor widow.

When he looked up he saw some wealthy people putting their offerings into the treasury and he noticed a poor widow putting in two small coins. He said, "I tell you truly, this poor widow put in more than all the rest; for those others have all made offerings from their surplus wealth, but she, from her poverty, has offered her whole livelihood." (Luke 21:1-4,NAB)

He is saying that we should not only give the minimum, but we should give sacrificially.

What does that mean? Well, it is different for each one of us. If your name is Bill Gates and you are worth seventy billion dollars, what would it mean to give ten percent away? Ten percent of seventy billion translates to seven billion dollars which is a lot of money. That would then leave him with sixty-three billion dollars to live off of – not quite resembling the widow's mite. In truth, he could reverse the tithe and give away ninety percent of his wealth and still be living high off the hog.

In determining how much we should give, we need to get away from legalistic formulas. Tithing charts can be a great first step, but we need to go deeper. Maybe you do not give that much to church or charity, but you are raising seven kids on a modest income. Perhaps you have taken in elderly parents or are supporting your neighbor in need. All of this should be factored in. The point is to be generous – to give until it hurts – to trust in God's providence. This is always much easier said than done. I am living proof of that.

Does all of this mean that we have to give up everything and live in a cardboard box? No. Nor do I think there is anything wrong about spending some money on leisure, travel or vacations. Likewise, being responsible by putting money away for college, retirement or savings. We just need to guard against excess, gluttony and greed. These conditions can easily creep in unless we are diligent. We need to be continually open to God's spirit, wisdom and guidance as it relates to our finances and what He is asking us to do with them. Do we own our possessions or do our possessions own us? The best answer is neither. God is the owner of all that we possess. We are just the stewards of the gifts he has given to us. Do you remember the rich young man?

Now someone approached him and said, "Teacher, what good must I do to gain eternal life?" He answered him, "Why do you ask me about the good? There is only One who is good. If you wish to enter into life, keep the commandments." He asked him, "Which ones?" And Jesus replied. You shall not kill; you shall not commit adultery; you shall not steal; you shall not bear false witness; honor your father and your mother; and you shall love your neighbor as yourself." The young man said to him, "All of these I have observed. What do I still lack?" Jesus said to him, "If you wish to be perfect, go, sell what you have and give to the poor, and you will have treasure in heaven. Then come, follow me." When the young man heard this statement, he went away sad, for he had many possessions.

*Then Jesus said to his disciples, "Amen I say to you, it will
be hard for one who is rich to enter the kingdom of heaven.
Again I say to you, it is easier for a camel to pass through
the eye of a needle than for one who is rich to enter the
kingdom of God." (Matthew 19:16-24, NAB)*

You notice that Jesus did not say to the rich young
man "Wait, don't leave. Perhaps I came on too strong
there. Let's talk about this some more. Maybe we can
work something out." No, he let him walk away sad.
Why? Of course, that is anyone's guess. My theory is
that the young man needed to be convicted of his sin
of greed. He needed to be challenged so that he
would have a change of heart and repent at some
point. In his particular case, it was not OK to hang on
to his money. His possessions now owned him and he
needed to let go to have life in Christ. Again, that
does not mean we need to sell all that we have, but
this story illustrates the significance of what we hold
dear. If we cling too tightly, God may be asking us to
release. How much and in what ways will be different
for each one of us.

Remember that everything we have is a gift from
God. Our charge is to be a responsible steward of
those gifts – not only to meet our own needs, but to be
a blessing to others. Keep asking God for ongoing
guidance and direction as He molds you into the
cheerful giver He has called you to be!

Service Stretching

A few years ago, I was helping with a retreat for juniors in a nearby Catholic high school. I was leading a small group discussion as we challenged the teens to go deeper in their faith. The conversation centered around a question that I posed to them. What does it mean to practice our faith? We hear that phrase tossed around a lot, but what does it really mean? I asked them to give me examples.

As expected, they threw out the standard responses. Going to Mass. Reading the Bible. Praying the Rosary. Because of the retreat theme, I was angling for some kind of response about volunteering or serving others and yet nothing like that came up. I kept prodding them and they still did not bring up anything related to service. Finally, after several obvious hints, one of the kids blurted out "Helping others." This exchange highlighted an undertone within our Catholic culture.

Even though the word itself "practicing" is very action oriented, many of us do not automatically think of serving others when asked the question. Most of us go straight to Mass attendance. After that, it is usually some kind of private prayer/devotion. Of course, that is true, but our faith involves so much more than that. We receive the Eucharist at Mass to then be Eucharist to the world. What was troubling about the student responses is that the motto for the school was "Seek to serve." These were juniors in their third year. So even when their motto is all about serving, they did not think of service to others as a critical part of practicing their faith.

It is not enough to simply pray or read spiritual books. Christ makes it pretty clear that we are to be His hands and feet in the world. Just take a look at the chilling words in The Judgment of the Nations that Jesus describes.

When the Son of Man comes in his glory, and all the angels with him, he will sit upon his glorious throne, and all the nations will be assembled before him. And he will separate them from one another, as a shepherd separates the sheep from the goats. He will place the sheep on his right and the goats on his left. Then the king will say to those on his right, "Come, you who are blessed by my Father. Inherit the kingdom prepared for you from the foundation of the world. For I was hungry and you gave me food, I was thirsty and you gave me drink, a stranger and you welcomed me, naked and you clothed me, ill and you cared for me, in prison and you visited me." Then the righteous will answer him and say, "Lord, when did we see you hungry and feed you, or thirsty and give you drink? When did we see you a stranger and welcome you, or naked and clothe you? When did we see you ill or in prison, and visit you?" And the king will say to them in reply, "Amen, I say to you, whatever you did for one of these least brothers of mine, you did for me." Then he will say to those on his left,

"Depart from me, you accursed, into the eternal fire prepared for the devil and his angels. For I was hungry and you gave me no food, I was thirsty and you gave me no drink, a stranger and you gave me no welcome, naked and you gave me no clothing, ill and in prison, and you did not care for me." Then they will answer and say, "Lord, when did we see you hungry or thirsty or a stranger or naked or ill or in prison, and not minister to your needs?" He will answer them, "Amen, I say to you, what you did not do for one of these least ones, you did not do for me." And these will go off to eternal punishment, but the righteous to eternal life." (Matthew 25:31-46, NAB)

Jesus makes a very bold statement here. Serving others is not simply "an extra" or optional. It is core to who we are as Catholics.

The title of this section contains the word stretching. In the workout world, stretching can be a challenging and painful activity. It is not easy or comfortable to try and stretch beyond our current limits. Serving others can definitely bring us far beyond our normal comfort zones.

One of the areas that can be challenging is in regards to social justice. Just the mention of the phrase may already be raising the hair on the back of your neck. For many politically or religiously conservative individuals, the term social justice conjures up images of leftist extremists who only want to save the trees and to strip away all remnants of capitalism. This is very unfortunate. Of course there are always going to be people on the fringe who advocate for things in the name of social justice that we may not agree with. However, it would be an absolute tragedy to throw the baby out with the bath water. When you think about it, Jesus was considered way too liberal (too radical) in what he did, thought, taught and proposed in comparison to the conservative religious leaders of the day who were simply trying to uphold and defend the Law. To be honest, I could see myself as being one of those Pharisees who would be criticizing Jesus when he picked grain on the Sabbath or claimed he was the Son of God.

Unlike many Protestant Evangelical churches, the Catholic Church cannot be pigeon-holed into nice, neat categories. We are not Democrat or Republican nor are we Liberal or Conservative. It really depends on the particular issue. On some social issues like abortion and euthanasia, we are considered very conservative. In others like environmental protection or trying to help the poor, we are considered quite liberal. We are consistently pro-life. From womb to tomb, we are called to protect and defend life in all of its stages. We are asked to create a world that is just and honors the dignity of each human person. This is a tall order. It is messy and complicated. It is difficult and challenging. Oftentimes, we do not see any impact because results are long term. And yet, our

Lord is asking us to make a difference in the world. This is not a political stance. This is not about taking sides or becoming liberal or conservative. This is about answering our baptismal call to live like Jesus did. It is beyond any human label or construct. It is about manifesting His radial love for all humankind.

There is a frequently told parable of unknown origin that is sometimes called "Babies in the River." This age old story has many different variations. Allow me to share one of my favorite versions that I oftentimes discuss with the teens.

There was a guy relaxing in his easy chair in his back yard which backed up to a river. Everything was quiet and serene until he heard screams coming from the water. In peering down the bank of the river, he noticed that a young child was floating downstream struggling to stay afloat. This poor kid was drowning. Immediately, he ran down the steep embankment and jumped in to rescue the child. After considerable effort and energy, he was able to reach the victim and pull the boy to safety. The man lay on the bank panting heavily from the scary situation that he and the child just escaped from. He and his wife were able to determine that the kid belonged to the child care center upstream. The little boy was returned safe and sound.

After the man had showered, he returned to his spot in the backyard to unwind from the stressful incident. Before he could get very comfortable, he heard another scream coming from the water. He peered down to see a different child in the same predicament. Again, he jumped in without hesitation and fortunately, was able to save this second kid. He thought it rather bizarre that this could happen twice in one day. However, stranger things have happened. Case in point was the fact that this second child also came from the day care upstream. He was incredulous, but was just happy that it turned out OK and that he could return to his home. He cleaned up and then decided to go to bed.

The next night he was working in his shed when he heard what sounded like a child struggling in the water. As he glanced toward the river, sure enough, there was another kid drowning. He was getting used to this so he knew the depths of the water and how strong the current was. He rescued the child in record time. At this point, he suspects that this one also belongs to the same day care center and indeed, the little girl does. Instead of returning home, he asks if he can go in the back yard of the center. As he walks the perimeter, he notices a slight gap in the fence. On closer inspection, he determines that the children have been escaping out of this crevice and subsequently slipping down the steep hillside right into the river. He works with the daycare center to shore up the fence and there were no more potential drowning victims.

This is a simple illustration of charity vs. justice. The man jumping into the river to save the children was a classic example of charity. He met the immediate need. This is good and necessary to do. However, it was only a short term fix. The problem kept occurring because there was a systemic issue (the hole in the fence). He recognized the recurring challenge and decided it made more sense to get at the root of the problem. Once he identified the cause of the children falling in the river, he did what was necessary to help prevent it from happening again.

Initially, it might have been easier to jump in the water to save the child, but with a little more investigation and effort, he accomplished something so much better. This is how it can be in real world examples. The concept of teaching someone to fish instead of simply giving them fish is something that the Church always asks us to work towards. It is better for the individual, for us and for society at large.

This is not an either/or scenario. In most cases, we need both. If a child falls in the river, we need to respond with charity and save them, but we would be remiss if we did not also work towards helping the daycare secure their fence and overall safety/supervision to prevent the incident in the first place. We will need to provide homeless shelters, but we should also be working to support affordable housing initiatives. We should help stock the emergency food pantries, but at the same time work to help these same people with job skill training or better education. We are called to recycle our cans and plastic goods, but look at our lifestyles to see if we can simplify our consumption in the first place.

Working in the realm of charity is very important. However, we are called to more. We need to look deeper at the root causes of what keeps people poor, hungry, incarcerated or homeless. What can we do to create a just society where people can support themselves and their families? Some simply need more help to get there. We are talking about a hand-up, not merely a hand-out.

What I suggest is this. Pick something that you are extremely passionate about. In other words, when you think about some of the injustices and tragedies in our world, what breaks your heart? Maybe it is world hunger or lack of clean drinking water. Perhaps it is the number of women battered each year or the children who are sexually abused. How about unsafe conditions in some of our neighborhoods or the millions of babies who are aborted? It could be a situation in your own workplace, school or family.

Look around. There are no shortages of worthy causes.

Our world is in desperate need of God's love and grace. Discern the particular passion that God has placed on your heart and ask for His guidance as to what He would like to do with it. There are literally thousands of organizations and agencies trying to address the myriad of societal ills. I would begin with your own parish or diocese. They probably have a ministry related to your passion so you can jump right in. As part of your service, it is important to educate yourself about the issues. This will help you be a much better voter, advocate and change agent.

These are just some of the spiritual exercises that can and should be done. No matter what you do, it is important to prioritize this into your everyday life. Continually ask the Lord to reveal new and challenging ways for you to grow as His disciple.

Divine Diet

As we all know, working out needs to be augmented by a healthy diet. There are many ways to feed our soul, but the main course is always the Eucharist.

Imagine what would happen if we only ate once a month. We would grow weak and eventually die. Well, this is what happens to our souls when we don't receive the Eucharist regularly. It is God's gift to us for our spiritual nourishment. It provides us with His energy, inspiration and strength. I will hear people (Protestant and Catholic) expressing their desire to get close to Jesus. You cannot get any closer than actually consuming His body and blood in Holy Communion.

I think we have all been at a place where we have taken the Eucharist for granted. We get up in line, shuffle up to the priest and mindlessly say "Amen" as we receive Him in this most precious Sacrament.

If this is where you still find yourself, it is time for a shift in attitude. What if your local parish announced in a press conference that Jesus Christ himself would be appearing this Sunday in the flesh at your local church? Not only would people show up early, but the place would be jam packed. Everyone would be waiting and praying in joyful anticipation.

Guess what? Jesus does make an appearance in the flesh at your parish every time Mass takes place. We just forget. Let us instead remember and celebrate this awesome and miraculous reality. It is God's great feast for us to experience life and life eternal.

The Church says it is a serious sin to deliberately skip Mass on Sundays. This is not some old fashioned rule that came off the books during Vatican II. No, it is still the case. Why? Because going to Mass not only honors God on the Sabbath, but it is essential for our souls to be strong and healthy. Make sure you are partaking of the food that never dies.

7 SPIRITUALLY FIT FOR LIFE

It is one thing to make improvements for a while or for a season. It is quite another to do so for the long haul. Even in the spiritual world, you can see where some people can lose steam, get weary and bogged down in discouragement. Spiritual dryness may set in and a person can find themselves wandering the desert. Perhaps that is where you find yourself right now. Or maybe you have experienced arid spells before. Or you are not even sure of what I am referring to. Do not worry. They are bound to arrive for you at some point ☺.

These periods can be pronounced, prolonged and painful. When we are caught in the sandstorms of life, we so badly yearn for the oasis – those religious high points where we felt so refreshed and full of life. Where have they gone? Doubts and anxiety can set in. Anger, bitterness and loneliness may decide to pay a visit as well. Why would God allow this? Why does He seem so distant now? What have I done to deserve His wrath? Why the divine cold shoulder?

Welcome to the human race and the normal spiritual journey. I have not met one person who, if they have lived long enough, has not experienced some of this in their life. It is not only common, but I believe it is necessary and beneficial. "What???" you may ask – "How can this possibly be a good thing?"

I do not pretend to have all of the answers or to understand the mind of God. We just have to look around at those that have gone before us. The Israelites were on a high after their miraculous escape from Egypt only to find themselves wandering the desert for forty years. Jesus gets baptized and his reward is to go spend forty days with the scorpions and rattlers in the desert. Oh, and a not so friendly guy named Satan was pestering him there as well. St. John of the Cross wrote extensively about the Dark Night of the Soul. More recently was the release of the struggles that our beloved Mother Teresa had. While she was filled with God's joy and grace, she also wrestled with long bouts of loneliness and aching.

How could any of this be good? As the saints and mystics will tell us, there is a tremendous benefit to being able to identify with the suffering of Christ and to offer that up to the Lord. This spiritual pruning makes us stronger and healthier.

A few years ago, there was a bio-dome in the Midwest. This was a facility built by scientists to be a testing ground for several different experiments. How would various plants and animals fare under idyllic conditions? An interesting development occurred with the trees. With perfect conditions, the theory was that they would grow and thrive. What they got instead were weak imitations. The trees could practically be pushed over with very little exertion. Why?

Without the normal forces of nature, they were not challenged in any substantial way. In particular, there was no wind in this "perfect" environment. In most natural environments, there is a steady supply of wind that goes up and down in intensity. This constant pushing forces the tree to sink and spread its roots deeper and deeper. This also occurs during periods of drought. Both of these conditions actually strengthen the tree and help it weather storms as they come in. Without an extensive root system, the trees become pushovers.

That is what can happen with us humans. We can become pushovers to everything the world may throw at us. God wants us to sink our roots deeper into Him. If you are going through a dry time, then be even more persistent in seeking Him. Even if you still do not feel anything, the very act of persistence and commitment is what matters. Your character, will and commitment are being fortified. You no longer rely on spiritual highs. You begin to worship and honor God not because of any spiritual benefit to you, but because you know it is simply the right thing to do. This very shift takes you to the next level. A shallow Christian easily drifts away from God if they do not feel anything or get anything out of Mass or some other spiritual activity. A mature believer follows God no matter what. Their faith cannot be easily shaken. Their resolve to follow the Lord is ironclad.

This process of purification and testing may not be enjoyable, but if we want to make progress in the spiritual life, we must embrace what God sends us. Being spiritually fit for life does not necessarily entail new spiritual exercises. That is part of the strength training mode. No, this is more about a solidifying of the will. To forge ahead no matter what the storms of life bring. To love, honor and praise God through thick and thin.

It is very similar to a marriage. When two people first meet, they are head over heels in love. Emotion carries the day. Once the honeymoon phase is over, their love develops into something more substantial. Even when there are trying times and the romance has faded, the bond actually strengthens because love takes on a sacrificial nature. That is where the vows come to life. You remember them, don't you? I will love, honor and cherish them in good times <u>and</u> in bad, in sickness <u>and</u> in health, for richer <u>or</u> poorer. It is no longer what you get out of the relationship. It is what you can give in love to the other.

It is the same with our relationship with the Lord. No matter what, we are His and as long as we remain committed to Him; His grace will enable us to be spiritually fit for life.

8 BECOMING A PERSONAL TRAINER

We come to the last stage of the journey and that is
mentorship. As Catholics, we fall into the sin of
omission when we keep the beauty of our faith to
ourselves. This is where we can learn a lot from our
Protestant brothers and sisters. They actively share
their faith and what God is doing in their life.
Catholics tend to privatize their faith and keep it
inside. We justify our silence by saying "I evangelize
by my actions." We misuse the phrase that is
famously (although perhaps inaccurately) attributed
to St. Francis. "Preach the gospel at all times and
when necessary, use words." There is no doubt that
we must be authentic in the way we live our lives.
This does speak volumes. Our words will be
meaningless or worse yet, harmful, if we enter into
hypocrisy, saying one thing and doing another.

However, we are called to both. Share verbally and be a good witness. It is both/and, not either/or. Sound like a familiar mantra in this book? It should. Life can be so much easier when it is either/or. A full-fledged disciple goes all the way.

Now it is time to train others. Just like my college roommate inspired me and showed me the way to properly lift weights, I then have returned the favor to several people over the years. This has come in very brief ways like when I get into casual conversation with others at the gym. They see me train the way I do and then inquire as to what my routine is. They see the fruits of my efforts and want to know more.

This happened to me the other day. A young man approached me when I was doing bench press and asked what my diet was. Sheepishly he shared that his goal was to look like me. He admired my fitness level and how strong I appeared to be even though I was twenty years older than him. I was flattered by his humble admission and I spent the next fifteen minutes giving him a synopsis of what I ate and what I did for my workouts. In addition, I showed him how to mix up his routine with various techniques. We had a great exchange and he was very grateful for what I could offer him. He had a noticeable pep in his step as he continued on with his routine. He seemed very inspired and energized by our exchange.

Besides random occurrences with strangers, I have been even more intentional with our kids. I have instructed them more intensely as to correct ways to train. I know how beneficial this has all been for me and I cannot, in good conscience, keep this to myself.

How much more true that is when it comes to our spiritual life. We know that without God, we are completely lost. Many people fall into a hopeless, depressive state. Again, how could we, in good conscience, ever keep this to ourselves? The gospel is not only Good News. It is the best news possible. We need to be sharing it every chance we get.

We need to be opportunistic when it comes to sharing our faith. I oftentimes hear people say when boarding the plane, "I hope no one is sitting beside me – I want to have peace and quiet." I like my peace and quiet as well. However, this is too good an opportunity to squander. You can rest, read or relax anytime. God may be placing this person next to you as their opportunity to hear something transformative. You might be planting or watering that seed of faith within them.

Naturally, we do not want to be overly aggressive, offensive or pushy. If it is not meant to be, then so be it. You cannot force conversion. The key to successful evangelization is being in tune with the promptings of the Holy Spirit. Every person and circumstance is different. Timing is everything. Pray before, during and after every encounter. God will guide you and give you the right words. The important thing is to be a willing and enthusiastic ambassador of God's love and mercy.

Beyond initial evangelization, we are also called to train, teach and disciple others. First and foremost, we start with our own family members. The Church has stated emphatically that parents are the first and primary teachers of their own children. As a parish employee, we usually see the opposite. Most people think their job as Catholic parents is to sign up their child for faith formation classes or to get them to go to youth group or attend the retreat. Of course, those activities are important, but mean almost nothing if the parents themselves are not actively living the faith. I always tell the parents the best thing they can do for their child's faith is to live the faith themselves. This does not mean they have to be perfect. That is why we call it *practicing* our faith. None of us are perfect. We are all on the journey. What I am referring to is our commitment. If it is not important to us, then why would it be to our children?

At my parish, we had an open ended interview process for high school teens preparing for Confirmation. It was not designed to be a quiz or test of any sort. It was a forum intended to help the kids reflect on their faith and where it was headed. On numerous occasions, a teen would lament something to the effect, "If Confirmation is so important to my mom and dad, then why don't they practice the faith themselves?" What can you say to that? They see through the hypocrisy. We cannot simply drop them off at the church curb and "Let the professionals instill faith in them". It does not work that way. Parish programs are meant to reinforce what is being taught and practiced in the domestic church. Church employees or faith formation volunteers are not meant to be the substitute for the child's parents. They could never do so even if they wanted to. They are only there to compliment them.

If you are a parent, you must be the primary personal trainer for your own children. To a similar degree, this would apply to your grandchildren, nephews, nieces, etc. Obviously, there are some family members that are going to be really hard to reach. Perhaps it will have to be someone from the outside who opens their heart to God. Be open, attentive and opportunistic.

As I mentioned, beyond initial evangelizing, everyone needs discipleship. We need to actively educate, form, encourage and guide not only our children, but other fellow pilgrims on the journey. Probably the best way to do this is to simply share your own experiences complete with failures and successes. Whenever I facilitate a meeting, group or class, I always try and make small group discussion a priority. People love sharing their stories and struggles with one another.

Remember what God is saying to us as His children – SHARE. Our greatest gift is faith itself. If other people in your life had kept the gospel message to themselves, you would not be where you are today. For your sake and the sake of God's kingdom, please do not be a spiritual Scrooge ☺!

9 FINAL THOUGHTS

Congratulations! You have made it to the end of the book. I intentionally made it shorter and more concise so the length would not be a barrier. There was no need to go on and on. The concept of faith and putting it into practice has never really been that complicated. We, as humans, have just made it that way.

As I mentioned in the beginning, reading something is only the first step. You are now on the cusp of transformation. You hear about people having a life changing event. Absorbing the concepts here does not qualify. No, the only way it becomes life changing is when you put these spiritual ideas in action.

Learn from one of my friends. Jimmy is a talker. He loves to hear himself proclaim big plans and lofty goals. Jimmy continually says how he is going to quit smoking, lose weight and start exercising. He talks about getting right with God and reading more of the Bible. Jimmy says all of these things with passion and conviction. If you did not know him, you would be duly impressed with his enthusiastic and outward commitment to move forward in life. Sadly, this is not the case. He has been talking like this for years. Oh, he takes a baby step here and there, and then his fire quickly flames out. Jimmy never sticks with anything long enough to take hold. He is a slave to his impulses. He is chronically stuck. He is bogged down in mediocrity. Don't be like Jimmy.

For the love of God and everyone around you, do not set this book down and forget about it. Make this promise to yourself right now. Within the next twenty-four hours, you will write down your personal moments of inspiration and insight and come up with a concrete game plan to move forward. You will install at least one new discipline or habit into your EVERYDAY life. You will mark this time as a spiritual milestone because you will be going from one level to another. You will no longer be the same.

I want you to look back at this period in your life as being one of tremendous growth – a real game changer. Commit your life to the Lord in every way possible. Be bold. Be persistent. Be committed. From this moment forward, make a pledge to be Catholic to the core!

Made in the USA
Lexington, KY
14 November 2018